A Great Big Ugly Man Came Up and Tied His Horse to Me

A Great Big Ugly Man Came Up and Tied His Horse to Me

A Book of Nonsense Verse

ILLUSTRATED BY
WALLACE TRIPP

Little, Brown and Company
BOSTON   TORONTO

Fourteenth Printing

The poem "Not Me" by Shel Silverstein is reprinted by permission of *Playboy* magazine. Copyright © 1960 by Shel Silverstein.

Library of Congress Cataloging in Publication Data

Tripp, Wallace, comp.
    A great big ugly man came up and tied his horse to me.

    SUMMARY: A collection of nonsense poems which in-
cludes, "I do not like thee, Doctor Fell," "Moll-in-the-
Wad," "Mother, may I go and swim?", and many others.
    1. Children's poetry. 2. Nonsense verses.
[1. Nonsense verses] I. Title.
PZ8.3.T7GR   398.8   74-189265
ISBN 0-316-85280-5

PK

Published simultaneously in Canada by Little, Brown & Company (Canada) Limited

PRINTED IN THE UNITED STATES OF AMERICA

As I was standing in the street,
As quiet as could be,
A great big ugly man came up
And tied his horse to me.

I eat my peas with honey,
I've done it all my life,
They do taste kind of funny,
But it keeps them on the knife.

It's once I courted as pretty a lass,
As ever you did see;
But now she's come to such a pass,
She never will do for me.
She invited me to her own house,
Where oft I'd been before,
And she tumbled me into the hog-tub,
And I'll never go there any more.

A horse and a flea and three blind mice
Sat on a curbstone shooting dice.
The horse he slipped and fell on the flea.
The flea said, "Whoops, there's a horse on me."

As I was going o'er London Bridge,
I heard something crack;
Not a man in all England
Can mend that!

Nose, nose, jolly red nose,
And what gave thee that jolly red nose?
Nutmeg and ginger, cinnamon and cloves,
That's what gave me this jolly red nose.

Jerry Hall,
He is so small,
A rat could eat him,
Hat and all.

I do not love thee, Doctor Fell,
The reason why I cannot tell;
But this alone I know full well,
I do not love thee, Doctor Fell.
— *Thomas Brown*

Bryan O'Lin had no breeches to wear,
So he bought him a sheepskin to make him a pair:
With the skinny side out, and the woolly side in,
"O how nice and warm!" cried Bryan O'Lin.

Moll-in-the-wad and I fell out,
And what do you think it was all about?
I gave her a shilling, she swore it was bad,
It's an old soldier's button says Moll-in-the-wad.

Mother, may I go and swim?
Yes, my darling daughter.
Hang your clothes on yonder limb,
But don't go near the water.

The Slithergadee has crawled out of the sea.
He may catch all the others, but he won't catch me.
No you won't catch me, old Slithergadee,
You may catch all the others, but you wo—

— *Shel Silverstein*

Said the monkey to the donkey,
"What'll you have to drink?"
Said the donkey to the monkey,
"I'd like a swig of ink."

What a wonderful bird the frog are.
When he sit he stand almost;
When he hop, he fly almost.
He ain't got no sense hardly.
He ain't got no tail hardly either.
When he sit, he sit on what he ain't got almost.

A mouse in her room woke Miss Dowd,
She was frightened and screamed very loud,
Then a happy thought hit her —
To scare off the critter,
She sat up in bed and meowed.

Some friend must now, perforce,
Go forth and bid my boy
To saddle me my wooden horse,
For I mean to conquer Troy.

I had a little pony,
His name was Dapple Grey;
He would bring me to an alehouse
A mile out of my way.

I am His Highness' dog at Kew;
Pray tell me, sir, whose dog are you?
— *Alexander Pope*

There was an old man from Peru
Who dreamed he was eating his shoe.
He woke in a fright
In the middle of the night
And found it was perfectly true.

The common cormorant or shag
Lays eggs inside a paper bag.
The reason you will see no doubt
It is to keep the lightning out.
But what these unobservant birds
Have never noticed is that herds
Of wandering bears may come with buns
And steal the bags to hold the crumbs.

I will tell my own daddy when he comes home,
What little good work my mamma has done.
She has earned a penny, spent a groat,
And burned a hole in the child's new coat.

As I went over Lincoln bridge
I met Mister Rusticap;
Pins and needles on his back,
A-going to Thorney Fair.

Jolly Roger lived up a tree.
You climbed there by a rope.
I'd often go for a cup of tea,
Which he brewed up with soap.

Once I found a sock in mine.
It made me wince a bit.
But Roger told me, "Never mind,
The blamed thing doesn't fit."

Milkman, milkman, where have you been?
In buttermilk channel up to my chin,
I spilt my milk, and I spoilt my clothes,
And got a long icicle hung to my nose.

If you are a gentleman,
As I suppose you be,
You'll neither laugh nor smile
At the tickling of your knee.

29

There was an old woman, and what do you think?
She lived upon nothing but victuals and drink;
Victuals and drink were the chief of her diet,
And yet this old woman could never keep quiet.

There was a man, and his name was Dob,
And he had a wife, and her name was Mob,
And he had a dog, and he called it Cob,
And she had a cat, called Chitterabob.
    Cob, says Dob,
    Chitterabob, says Mob.
    Cob was Dob's dog,
    Chitterabob Mob's cat.

Bow, wow, wow,
Whose dog art thou?
Little Tom Tinker's dog,
Bow. Wow. Wow.

Hark! the herald angels sing,
Beecham's Pills are just the thing.
Peace on earth and mercy mild,
Two for man and one for child.

An epicure, dining at Crewe,
Found quite a large mouse ın his stew.
   Said the waiter, "Don't shout,
   And wave it about,
Or the rest will be wanting one, too!"

34

An old grey horse stood on the wall,
As daft as he was high.
He had no fear of falling down,
He thought he was a fly.

35

Dickery, dickery, dare,
The pig flew up in the air;
The man in brown soon brought him down,
Dickery, dickery, dare.

Ah, lovely Devon . . .
Where it rains eight days out of seven!

Rain on the green grass,
And rain on the tree,
Rain on the house-top,
But not on me.

For want of a nail the shoe was lost,
For want of a shoe the horse was lost,
For want of a horse the rider was lost,
For want of a rider the battle was lost,
For want of a battle the kingdom was lost.
And all for the want of a horseshoe nail.

Here lies the body of Jonathan Pound,
Who was lost at sea and never found.

I am a pretty wench,
And I come a great way hence,
And sweethearts I can get none:
But every dirty sow,
Can get sweethearts enow,
And I, pretty wench, can never get a one.

St. Dunstan, as the story goes,
Once pulled the devil by the nose,
With red hot tongs, which made him roar,
That could be heard ten miles or more.

Hannah Bantry, in the pantry,
Gnawing at a mutton bone;
  How she gnawed it,
  How she clawed it,
When she found herself alone.

Six little mice sat down to spin,
Pussy passed by and she peeped in.
What are you doing, my little men?
Making coats for gentlemen.
Shall I come in and cut off your threads?
No, no, Miss Pussy, you'll bite off our heads.
Oh, no, I'll not, I'll help you spin.
That may be so, but you don't come in.

Three little mice ran up the stairs
To hear Miss Blodgett say her prayers.

When Miss Blodgett said "Amen,"
The three little mice ran down again.

There was a rat, for want of stairs,
Went down a rope to say his prayers.

Truly, she doth block a staircase.

When I was a little Boy
I had but little Wit,
'Tis a long time ago,
And I have no more yet;

Nor ever, ever shall,
Until that I die,
For the longer I live,
The more Fool am I.

46